SHARING

OUR

LOVE

JOANNE FINK

8102 Lemont Road,
#300, Woodridge, IL 60517, U.S.A.
Phone: 630-390-3580   Fax: 630-390-3585

Compiled by Joanne Fink

Cover Design by Design Dynamics
Calligraphy by Joanne Fink

Published by Great Quotations, Inc.

ISBN: 1-56245-374-2

Printed in Hong Kong 2002

Love

is sharing all of the wonderful things life has to offer with the person you care most about.

Weave
the threads
of your lives
together with
Love.

Anything
is possible
if you do it
together!

THE PERFECT RELATIONSHIP

is more than finding the right person. It's **BEING** the right person.

A RELATIONSHIP
that grows
from mutual love
and respect,
kindness, understanding
and compassion
is strong enough
to last a lifetime.

The place
to be happy is here.

The time
to be happy
is now.

The way to be happy
is to make
another happy.

AUTHOR
UNKNOWN

Having someone
with whom
to laugh,
talk, cry and dream,
is having
a friend to love.

A caring relationship when nurtured can blossom into Love.

Delight

IN SPENDING

TIME WITH

THE PERSON

YOU LOVE.

Treat

EACH DAY
TOGETHER AS
A GIFT AND
AN ADVENTURE.

THE TEST
OF A LOVING
AND LASTING
RELATIONSHIP
LIES IN
COPING WITH
AND GROWING
FROM WHATEVER
DIFFICULTIES
MIGHT ARISE.

A friend

IS SOMEONE
WHO NOT ONLY
ACCEPTS YOU FOR
WHAT YOU ARE
BUT MAKES YOU
FEEL GOOD ABOUT
BEING YOURSELF.

Take the
time to give
to one another,
to work things
out together,
to talk, to listen and
to appreciate
each other.

AS YOU
WALK DOWN
LIFE'S PATH
TOGETHER,
Share your thoughts
AND UNITE
YOUR SPIRITS
IN Love.

LOVE IS
LISTENING TO WORDS SPOKEN AND TO THOSE LEFT UNSAID.

The one word
that makes
a partnership
successful is
'OURS'

Falling in love

is easy.

Growing in love

must be

worked at with

determination.

Lesley Barfoot

Couples who *Love*
each other
tell each other
a thousand
things
without talking.

CHINESE PROVERB

Happy
relationships
are built
on blocks
of patience.

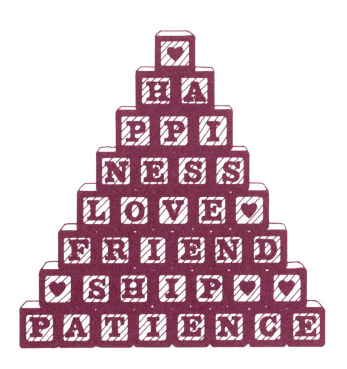

Friendship is the cement that holds a relationship together.

Author
Unknown

Love
follows
friendship
&
friendship
follows
Love

Never forget
THAT
THE MOST
POWERFUL
FORCE ON
EARTH IS
Love.

Nelson Rockerfeller

TWO HEARTS THAT SHARE ONE LOVE

will grow together in

JOY.

Lasting love is a
PROMISE
that takes a
lifetime
to fulfill.

The best way
to appreciate
a loved one
is to imagine
yourself
without them.

Without rain, there could be no RAINBOWS. Without sorrow, JOY would not be as sweet.

29

Most people
are about as
happy as they
make up
their minds to be.

Abraham Lincoln

Two souls
with but a
single thought;
two hearts
that beat as one.

Von Munch Billinghausen

A successful relationship REQUIRES HONESTY, INTEGRITY, COMMITMENT AND CARING.

Two people
who work
to bring out
the best in
each other
truly have a
committed
relationship.

LOVE

IS

FRIENDSHIP

that has
caught fire!

Ann Landers

Happiness

COMES
FROM A LOVE
THAT DEEPENS
WITH EVERY
PASSING DAY.

*Like a tree
in the
autumn wind,
it is better
to bend
than to break.*

LOVE
IS
SHARING
A PART OF
YOURSELF
WITH
OTHERS!

JANET HOFFBERG

In DREAMS
and in
Love
there are no
impossibilities.

JANUS ARONY

DREAMS

*When you
share a dream
you work
together to
make it happen.*

Fairytales are not just for children;

Dreams really do come true.

Love

is caring
more about
another person
than you
do about
yourself.

Love
endures only
when lovers
love many things
not merely
each other.

Walter Lippman

Love

makes me
want to sing
the melody
my heart
is playing!

A SMALL
HOUSE
*will hold
just as much
happiness
as a large one.*

AUTHOR
UNKNOWN

Love
is
a little word.
Those in love
make it big!

AUTHOR UNKNOWN

Love is
the master key
that opens
the gates of
HAPPINESS.

Oliver Wendell Holmes

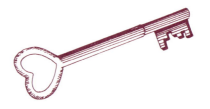

HAPPINESS
is the
feeling
that comes
from
sharing your
LOVE.

Let there
be spaces
in your
togetherness.

Kahlil Gibran

HOPE TOGETHER–

if it were not
for hope,
the heart
would break.

Unknown

Be honest
with each other.
But more
importantly
be honest
with yourself.

LOVE
DOES NOT CONSIST OF GAZING AT EACH OTHER BUT IN LOOKING OUTWARD TOGETHER IN THE SAME DIRECTION

ANTOINE DE SAINT-EXUPÉRY

INDIVIDUALS BRING THEIR OWN UNIQUE COLLECTION OF EXPERIENCES, MEMORIES, THOUGHTS AND IDEALS TO A RELATIONSHIP.

Those who
bring sunshine
into the lives
of others,
cannot keep it
from themselves!

James Barrie

57

FAITH,
TRUST
AND
FORGIVENESS
can work
wonders.

A HAPPY HOME

*expresses
a couple's
love for
one another.*

The foundation of
a happy home
comes from the
LOVE & TRUST
of the people who
live inside it.

61

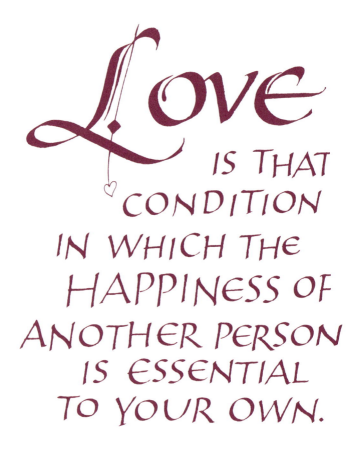

Love IS THAT CONDITION IN WHICH THE HAPPINESS OF ANOTHER PERSON IS ESSENTIAL TO YOUR OWN.

ROBERT HEINLEIN

TO LOVE
IS TO
PLACE
OUR
HAPPINESS
IN THE
HAPPINESS
OF ANOTHER.

GOTTFRIED VON LIEBNITZ

You CAN GIVE WITHOUT LOVING, BUT YOU CAN NEVER LOVE WITHOUT GIVING.

LOVE CAN FILL

HOMES WITH SONG

HEARTS WITH SMILES

AND DAYS WITH SUNSHINE

There are
so many
ways to love
and each one
has its own
delights!

Sara Teasdale

It takes
imagination
to make a
relationship
flourish.

The sun
*S*H*I*N*E*S*
so much
brighter
when
I see
your smile.

Love is
the quiet
understanding
and mature
acceptance
of imperfection.

Ann Landers

Nobody
is perfect.
COMPROMISE
is a necessary
part of any
relationship.

Love
AND
Imagination
make a
house a
Home.

I love
coming
home
BECAUSE
YOU ARE
THERE.

Loving you

IS THE
BEST THING
THAT EVER
HAPPENED
TO ME.

LOVE IS A GIFT

and yours is the best present I've ever gotten.

Friendship

IS ONE OF

THE NICEST

KINDS OF

Love!

Other Titles by Great Quotations, Inc.

Hard Covers

Ancient Echoes
Behold the Golfer
Commanders in Chief
The Essence of Music
First Ladies
Good Lies for Ladies
Great Quotes From Great Teachers
Great Women
I Thought of You Today
Journey to Success
Just Between Friends
Lasting Impressions
My Husband My Love
Never Ever Give Up
The Passion of Chocolate
Peace Be With You
The Perfect Brew
The Power of Inspiration
Sharing the Season
Teddy Bears
There's No Place Like Home

Paperbacks

301 Ways to Stay Young
ABC's of Parenting
Angel-grams
African American Wisdom
Astrology for Cats
Astrology for Dogs
The Be-Attitudes
Birthday Astrologer
Can We Talk
Chocoholic Reasonettes
Cornerstones of Success
Daddy & Me
Erasing My Sanity
Graduation is Just the Beginning
Grandma I Love You
Happiness is Found Along the Way
Hooked on Golf
Ignorance is Bliss
In Celebration of Women
Inspirations
Interior Design for Idiots

Great Quotations, Inc.
8102 Lemont Road,
#300, Woodridge, IL 60517, U.S.A.
Phone: 630-390-3580   Fax: 630-390-3585

Other Titles by Great Quotations, Inc.

Paperbacks

I'm Not Over the Hill
Life's Lessons
Looking for Mr. Right
Midwest Wisdom
Mommy & Me
Mother, I Love You
The Mother Load
Motivating Quotes
Mrs.Murphy's Laws
Mrs. Webster's Dictionary
Only A Sister
The Other Species
Parenting 101
Pink Power
Romantic Rhapsody
The Secret Langauge of Men
The Secret Langauge of Women
The Secrets in Your Name
A Servant's Heart
Social Disgraces
Stress or Sanity
A Teacher is Better Than
Teenage of Insanity
Touch of Friendship
Wedding Wonders
Words From the Coach

Perpetual Calendars

365 Reasons to Eat Chocolate
Always Remember Who Loves You
Best Friends
Coffee Breaks
The Dog Ate My Car Keys
Extraordinary Women
Foundations of Leadership
Generations
The Heart That Loves
The Honey Jar
I Think My Teacher Sleeps at School
I'm a Little Stressed
Keys to Success
Kid Stuff
Never Never Give Up
Older Than Dirt
Secrets of a Successful Mom
Shopoholic
Sweet Dreams
Teacher Zone
Tee Times
A Touch of Kindness
Apple a Day
Golf Forever
Quotes From Great Women
Teacher Are First Class